COMMANDING MY MORNING

PRAYERS TO CONDITION MY DAY

FAITH & WORKS
MINISTRIES

Faith & Works Ministries
+1 721 526 8363
faithandworks.sxm@gmail.com
www.faithandworks.church
Sint Maarten Dutch West Indies

Copyright ©2023 by Ivon Valerie

All rights reserved. No part of this book may be reproduced, stored in a retrieval system, or transmitted in any form or by any means, electronic, mechanical, photocopying, recording, scanning, or otherwise, without the publisher's prior written permission.

New International Version (NIV) copyright © 1973, 1978, 1984, 2011 by Biblica, Inc.® Used by permission. All rights reserved worldwide.

King James Version (KJV) public domain

New Living Translation (NLT) are taken from the Holy Bible, New Living Translation, copyright ©1996, 2004, 2015 by Tyndale House Foundation. Used by permission of Tyndale House Publishers, Carol Stream, Illinois 60188. All rights reserved.

ESV® Bible (The Holy Bible, English Standard Version®), copyright © 2001 by Crossway, a publishing ministry of Good News Publishers. Used by permission. All rights reserved. The ESV text may not be quoted in any publication made available to the public by a Creative Commons license. The ESV may not be translated in whole or in part into any other language.

ISBN: **9798378617326**
SAPIENTIAL PUBLISHING
Cover & Interior design by Ivon Valerie
First edition: February 2023
Second edition: July 2023

Faith & Works Ministries

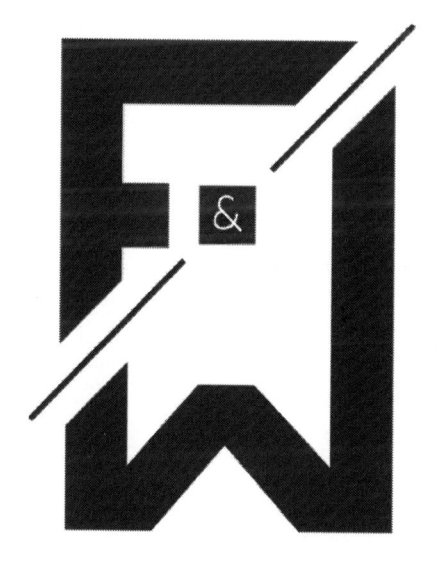

Prayers To Condition My Day

Table of Content

About Faith & Works Ministries -------------------------7

Introduction ---11

Humility--15

The Word of God --------------------------------------16

Say What God Is Saying (Thus Says the Lord)-------17

Purity --18

Pray Specific Prayers ----------------------------------19

Worship--23

Confessions---27

General Prayer Points ---------------------------------33

Prayer Points for Praying for Your Child(Ren) --------51

Welcome to our Family---------------------------------59

Commanding My Morning

ABOUT FAITH & WORKS MINISTRIES

Faith & Works Ministries is a faith-based organization dedicated to creating a nurturing and supportive environment for individuals who seek to live out their faith through service to God and others. We aim to empower our community members to embrace biblical principles and apply them to their daily lives meaningfully. We believe that a life of faith is not just about personal salvation but also about positively impacting others and the world around us.

To achieve our mission, we strive to create a welcoming community that values diversity, respect, and compassion. We offer a range of ministries, programs, and activities designed to help individuals deepen their relationship with God, discover their unique talents and callings, and use them to serve God and others. Our worship experiences are designed to inspire and uplift, while our relevant teachings provide practical guidance on applying biblical principles to everyday life. Additionally, our training programs equip individuals with the skills and knowledge they need to serve others effectively. Our love and compassionate care initiatives ensure that those in need receive the support and assistance they require.

At Faith & Works Ministries, we are guided by the belief that faith without works is dead. We encourage our community members to not only talk about their faith but also to put it into action by serving God and others with love and kindness. We believe doing so can make a positive difference in the world and bring glory to God. Whether it's through volunteering at a local shelter, mentoring a young person, or simply offering a kind word to someone in need, every act of service has the power to transform lives and communities. Ultimately, our goal is to create a world where individuals are empowered to live out their faith in tangible ways, and everyone can experience God's love and compassion.

Apostle Ivon Valerie
Faith & Works Ministries

Prayers To Condition My Day

Introduction

Welcome to '**Commanding My Morning: Prayers to Condition My Day**.' This guide will assist you in experiencing God's best every day. God desires to bless and prosper you, but the devil and his agents work tirelessly to fill your day with evil. The enemy aims to steal all God has in store for you today. Jesus, as mentioned in the Bible, also practiced commanding His mornings, "In the morning before the sun was up, Jesus went to a place where He could be alone. He prayed there." (Mark 1:35). By following God's instructions and beginning your day with commands, prayers, and declarations, you are taking proactive measures against any potential negative influences or plans the enemy may have set in motion to sabotage what God has in store for you.

In the Book of Job, God poses a thought-provoking inquiry to Job, questioning whether he has ever commanded the morning and instructed the dawn to know its place. This question is a powerful reminder to begin each day positively, setting the tone for the day ahead. Doing so effectively counteracts any unfavorable circumstances that may arise throughout the day. It is essential to approach each new day with a mindset of purpose and positivity, as it can significantly impact the outcomes of our daily experiences.

The early hours present an excellent opportunity to pray and set the tone for the rest of your day. As highlighted in Romans 12:2, it is important to resist the temptation to conform to the world's ways and instead focus on renewing our minds and seeking God's will. By taking control of our thoughts and emotions at the start of each day, we can assert our authority over our lives and prevent negative influences from taking hold. This practice of "commanding the morning" is a powerful way to approach each new day with purpose and positivity.

Commencing your day with powerful commands, declarations, and prayer points is a highly effective way to align your thoughts and actions with God's divine will and purpose for your life. This practice can bring greater peace, clarity, and direction throughout your day and strengthen your faith and reliance on God. Reciting these declarations can offer additional protection and guidance, which is especially vital in times of uncertainty and adversity.

Prayers To Condition My Day

As stated in Isaiah 58:11, "The Lord will guide you always; he will satisfy your needs in a sun-scorched land and will strengthen your frame. You will be like a well-watered garden, like a spring whose waters never fail." This powerful verse reminds us of God's unwavering love and support for us, even in the toughest of times.

Commanding your morning is particularly impactful if done between midnight and 3:00 am. It is a powerful way to ward off any evil plans that may have been set against you and claim authority over your day. The effectiveness of commands heavily depends on the character of the person issuing them. Commands serve the purpose of providing clear and direct guidance toward achieving a desired outcome or objective. They are also used to establish boundaries and expectations. However, despite their seemingly straightforward nature, commands are not always followed. One reason for this is a lack of respect.

Respect is a crucial component of effective command-giving. The person issuing the commands must be respected by the person following them. Obedience is not simply mindlessly following directions; it also involves understanding them and being willing to comply. This understanding and willingness to comply must stem from a place of respect. When respect is present, the commands will be followed with greater ease and effectiveness, leading to a more productive and successful outcome.

To effectively command one's mornings, one must understand that respect and obedience are earned through personal character. A person with a strong character is honest, reliable, and accountable, always following through on their promises. They are trustworthy and dependable, making them natural authority figures that others look up to and respect.

The importance of possessing good characteristics cannot be overstated, particularly when commanding obedience and respect from others. This is especially true when issuing morning commands, as it sets the tone for the rest of the day. While the words used in issuing commands are important, one's lifestyle is even more critical. Cultivating a positive and robust character will make morning commands all the more effective, as you will be seen as someone that can be trusted and followed.

Good character traits also have a profound impact on the spirit realm. The biblical account of the seven sons of Sceva in Acts 19:14-16 highlights this. Despite using the right words to command evil spirits, their lack of good and Godly characteristics made their commands ineffective. Therefore, it is imperative to cultivate specific qualities such as humility and purity to effectively command our mornings and earn respect in all aspects of life.

HUMILITY

It is imperative to approach each morning with humility to take control of your day effectively. This approach enables you to recognize that you are not the ultimate authority and require the help of God, who possesses limitless power. Humility allows you to acknowledge your limited strength, wisdom, and abilities and seek God's guidance and protection. Understanding our limitations and recognizing God's All-powerfulness can give us a proper perspective of our role and relationship with God.

Furthermore, humility allows us to submit to God's authority, as it is stated in James 4:6 that "God opposes the proud but gives grace to the humble." Apostle Peter also reminds us in 1 Peter 5:5 that "God is opposed to the proud, but gives grace to the humble." By being humble, we position ourselves to receive God's grace and blessings and have stronger faith in God. Cultivating humility is critical to taking control of your day, submitting to God's authority, and strengthening your faith in God.

THE WORD OF GOD

Understanding the importance of God's word and its application is paramount when commanding our mornings effectively. The Bible teaches us that God's word is "alive and active, sharper than any double-edged sword" (Hebrews 4:12). By internalizing this truth and storing it in our hearts (Psalm 119:11), we equip ourselves to avoid sinning against God. Through the laws and principles outlined in the Bible, we can arm ourselves against the enemy's tactics and use this knowledge to our advantage when standing firm in our faith.

Another crucial aspect of commanding our mornings is understanding who we are in Christ. The Bible tells us that we are "in Christ Jesus" (Romans 8:1), and as a result, we are a "new creation" (2 Corinthians 5:17). This means that our past mistakes and failures no longer define us. With our new identity in Christ and His power, we can confidently stand against the enemy's attacks and live a fulfilling life.

As believers, we can experience true victory. Romans 8:37 assures us we are "more than conquerors through him who loved us." This knowledge empowers us to speak with authority in the morning, knowing that living according to God's Word brings effectiveness. With the power of Christ within us, we can face any challenge with strength and courage.

To command our mornings effectively, we must know and understand the Word of God and live it out in our daily lives. By familiarizing ourselves with the laws and principles outlined in scripture and applying them to our lives, we fortify ourselves against the enemy's attacks and use them to our advantage. Relying on the power of Christ within us, we can strengthen ourselves against the enemy and live confidently in our new identity.

SAY WHAT GOD IS SAYING (THUS SAYS THE LORD)

One of the most powerful ways to start your day is by confidently speaking God's words. When you do so, you are exercising a spiritual authority that comes from the teachings of the Lord. The phrase "Thus saith the Lord" holds immense power in the spiritual realm because God's word is always right and true; He is faithful in all He does.

The Bible tells us that God's word is alive, active, and sharper than any double-edged sword. Speaking God's word helps us to align with His will and purpose for our lives, but we must first understand His teachings. This is why it is essential to consistently study and analyze the scriptures so that we can "study to show ourselves approved unto God, a workman that needeth not to be ashamed, rightly dividing the word of truth" (2 Timothy 2:15).

Starting your day with purpose requires having steadfast and unwavering faith. Scripture teaches us that "the kingdom of God suffers violence and the violent take it by force" (Matthew 11:12). This indicates that actively claiming God's promises and blessings with strong and fervent faith is essential. This can be achieved by speaking God's promises over your life and standing firm in your faith, even when faced with challenges.

Furthermore, the Bible instructs us to "resist the devil, and he will flee from you" (James 4:7) and reveals that "the weapons of our warfare are not of the flesh but have divine power to destroy strongholds" (2 Corinthians 10:4). Each morning, by approaching the day with courageous faith, we actively engage in spiritual warfare, fighting against the devil and using God's divine power to overcome any obstacles that may come our way. Therefore, we must always be vigilant and steadfast in our faith, trusting God's promises and teachings to guide us through every moment.

PURITY

In today's society, finding individuals who possess the quality of purity is becoming increasingly rare. However, this quality is crucial when successfully commanding your morning. Living a pure and holy life is necessary to have a greater possibility of success when we issue commands. The teachings of the Bible stress the importance of holiness, as it is stated that without it, we cannot see the Lord (Hebrews 12:14). Additionally, it is emphasized that God's holy people must lead a pure life in all aspects (1 Peter 1:15). Striving for purity and holiness in our daily lives enables us to align ourselves with God's will, granting us authority in the spiritual realm. We must understand that in the spirit realm, purity is power.

It's worth noting that purity of heart is a blessing in itself, as the Bible reminds us that the pure in heart will see God (Matthew 5:8). By cultivating a pure heart, we can see God more clearly and love and help others more effectively. Ultimately, purity aligns us with God's will, granting us greater spiritual authority. Therefore, we must strive for purity in all our lives to succeed and harmonize with God's will.

PRAY SPECIFIC PRAYERS

When you come before God to make your requests and command your day, it is crucial that you approach your time with intentionality and specificity in your prayers and commands. James 4:2 reminds us that we may only receive what we desire if we ask for it. You must articulate your needs and concerns to God through specific prayers to position yourself to receive His blessings.

To ensure that you start your day on the right footing, it's critical to incorporate various elements into your morning routine, including commands, declarations, and prayers. To do this effectively, you must strive to live in humility, abide in the Word of God, understand your identity in Christ Jesus, speak what God says, and maintain unwavering faith. Prioritizing purity and praying to remain connected with God and receive His blessings is also crucial. Following these guidelines can strengthen your relationship with God and enable you to experience His abundant benefits.

So, as you begin the commanding of your day, take the time to be intentional and specific in your prayers and commands, and trust that God will hear and answer you according to His will. With these guiding principles, you can step forward confidently into the day ahead, knowing that God is with you and leading you every step of the way.

Prayers To Condition My Day

Prayers To Condition My Day

Worship

Expressing gratitude and reverence towards God is paramount and should be considered a fundamental aspect of commanding your morning.

SING ALONG TO WORSHIP MUSIC AND LIFT THE KING OF KINGS AND LORD OF LORDS IN PRAISE.

AFTER OR DURING OR TIME OF WORSHIP AND PRAISE, PRAY THIS PRAYER.

Dear Father,

I humbly come before you; I cannot help but feel an immense reverence and admiration for your divine nature and infinite wisdom. You are the creator of the heavens and the earth, and your love and grace know no bounds. As your devoted child and loyal subject, I am forever grateful for your unwavering love and for adopting me into your divine family.

I give thanks for the sacrifice of your beloved son, Jesus, who laid down his life for me on the cross at Calvary. Through his selfless act of love, I have been redeemed and reconciled to you, my Abba, Father. Through him, I can confidently approach your throne of grace and experience the fullness of life as your child.

I am grateful for the great honor of being a joint heir with Christ Jesus. Your all-powerful nature humbles me, and the authority and privilege you have given me over all the works of your hands are deeply appreciated and cherished. I have been given a new name and authority through your infinite wisdom and mercy in heaven and on earth.

Your constant love, grace, and faithfulness toward me are truly remarkable, and I acknowledge them with immense gratitude. As stated in 1st Peter 2:9, you have graciously made me a Royal Priest and a unique person, chosen to be a part of a holy nation, your special possession. I am eternally grateful for the power and authority to proclaim your praises and truth.

According to the Scriptures, "What is man that you are mindful of him, and the son of man that you visit him? For you have made him have dominion over the works of your hands; you have put all things under his feet." (Psalms 8:5&6) At the beginning of creation, you commanded all heavenly hosts and creations to hear your word regarding my existence. You, the sovereign King, said, "Let us make man in our image, after our likeness, and let them have dominion over the fish of the sea, and over the fowl of the air, and the cattle, and all the earth, and over every creeping thing that creeps on the earth." (Genesis 1:26)

As I claim my authority in Christ Jesus and assert my rightful dominion over the elements, I am mindful of the importance of taking charge of my mornings and guiding the day-springs to their rightful places to rid the earth of wickedness, as stated in Job 38:12&13. Therefore, I am commanding the day-spring to its proper position this morning. I am also asking for the protection of myself, my family, my possessions, my dreams, my aspirations, my ministry, my destiny, and Faith & Works Ministries through the covering of the blood of Jesus.

May my words and actions always reflect your love and truth as I strive to live by your divine will. I am forever grateful for the power and authority you have given me as your cherished creation, and I will continue to honor and glorify your Holy name in all that I do.

-Amen

Confessions

This beautiful morning, I am finding solace and tranquility in the powerful words of Psalms 5:1-3. This verse reminds me that the Lord always listens to my thoughts and prayers. I am confident that He is listening to my cries and petitions. As I offer my supplications to my King and God, I am reassured that He will continue to guide me through all my trials and tribulations.

Also comforting is Psalms 121:1-8, which emphasizes that my help comes only from the Lord, the Creator of heaven and earth. As I gaze upon the hills with faith and hope, I am filled with the knowledge that He will always protect me and keep me from stumbling. The Lord never sleeps nor slumbers and is always watching over me. He is my keeper and shade, shielding me from the scorching sun and the moon's piercing light. He protects me from all evil, safeguarding my soul and ensuring my safety.

In all my comings and goings, I trust that the Lord will always be there for me, preserving and keeping me safe. His unwavering love and care give me the strength to face each new day and overcome all obstacles that come my way. May His mercy and grace continue to shine upon me, now and always.

Finding comfort in living within the hidden sanctuary of God and remaining under His unwavering protection is where I place my trust. For He is my rock and my salvation, and in Him, I find refuge and fortitude. Whenever I find myself ensnared by the traps of the enemy or succumb to dreadful afflictions, God rescues me. His sheltering wings envelop me, and I believe in their power and safety.

My defense is rooted in the truth of the Lord, and I am unafraid of any dangers that may arise during the day or night or of any destruction that may come at noon, for God is my protector. Even if a thousand of my enemies were to attack my side or ten thousand on my right, I remain confident that no harm will come to me. I am assured that I will only witness the punishment of the wicked with my own eyes. I am convinced that no evil or plague will come near my dwelling place because I have taken refuge in the Lord.

My God and King commands His angels to watch over me and protect me in all my ways. They are to lift me in their hands in case I stumble. I am emboldened to declare that I now walk over lions and snakes and confidently trample over young lions and dragons. As I call upon God this morning, I proclaim that He will answer me, for He is with me in times of trouble and will rescue and honor me. I am content with a long and fulfilling life because God has revealed His salvation to me.

Believers will find it helpful to recite these positive biblical affirmations below to strengthen their faith and fight against the negative influence of the devil. These declarations can be a powerful tool to reinforce your core beliefs and values, ultimately providing a sense of fortitude and protection during times of spiritual challenge.

1. I have been saved from the devil's grasp by the redeeming and cleansing power of the blood of Jesus. His sacrifice has granted me salvation and freedom from the darkness that once consumed me.

2. I am filled with an unwavering sense of assurance that the precious blood of our Lord and Savior, Jesus Christ, is at work within me at all times, purifying me of all my past and present wrongs and granting me eternal salvation.

3. Through the sacrificial and redemptive power of Jesus' blood, I am entirely absolved of all wrongdoing and deemed righteous in the eyes of God. It is as if I have never transgressed or sinned, and I can confidently stand before the Lord without fear of condemnation.

4. I am incredibly grateful for the selfless and ultimate sacrifice made by Jesus Christ. I am now filled with the divine holiness of God, which brings me great comfort, peace, and a sense of purpose. This profound transformation has truly changed my life, and I feel blessed to have been allowed to experience it.

5. The invaluable and sacred blood of our Lord and Savior, Jesus Christ, is graciously interceding on my behalf in the heavenly realms, affording me the uninterrupted privilege of receiving and experiencing God's boundless and unfailing love through His merciful forgiveness.

6. I am grateful for the unparalleled honor of accessing the most sacred and revered realm in all of existence, where I am granted the opportunity to stand before the all-powerful Creator of the universe. This incredible privilege is bestowed upon me only because of the precious and holy blood of Jesus, which has been lovingly and mercifully sprinkled for me. It is a profound

and humbling experience that fills me with overwhelming admiration and gratitude.

Prayers To Condition My Day

THESE PRAYER POINTS CAN HELP YOU TAKE COMMAND OF YOUR DAY EFFECTIVELY. THESE PRAYER POINTS SERVE MERELY AS A GUIDE; ALLOWING GOD TO GUIDE YOUR PRAYERS AND COMMANDS IS VERY IMPORTANT AND ENCOURAGED.

General Prayer Points

1. Dear God, I wake up early to acknowledge your sovereignty. I humbly seek refuge and blessings from the sacred anointing of the early morning. I proclaim Your magnificence with reverence and gratitude. Please reveal to me secrets that will manifest the decrees of heaven on earth.

2. I command the morning to open its ears to me and hear my cry.

3. I demand that my directives be given prompt attention and executed immediately to achieve the desired results.

4. I command the earth to get in place and receive heavenly instructions on my behalf.

5. I command that heavenly resources are favoring me today.

6. I command that this is the day the Lord has made; I will rejoice and be glad.

7. I command all the elements of this day to cooperate with me in the name of Jesus.

8. I command the elemental forces to refuse to cooperate with my enemies today.

9. This morning, I demand that all the elements of creation obey my commands without hesitation.

10. I declare that as my praise and prayers resound and the day breaks, the earth will yield her increase to me.

11. I decree that the first fruit of my morning is holy, so my entire day is holy.

12. I prophesy the will of God to the morning so that the day-spring (dawn) will know its place in my days.

13. I decree that I am strategically lined up with the ladder that touches heaven and sits on earth. Even now, angels are descending and ascending according to my words.

14. This morning, I pray for protection for myself and my family from any harm from the sun, moon, and stars. I ask for harmony between the elements and the heavenly hosts so that we may receive God's blessings and favor.

15. I command that any negative energy planning to work against my life today will be brought down, disgraced, and nullified in the name of Jesus.

16. I dismantle any power contrary to the will of God that is uttering incantations to capture this day.

17. I render null and void such incantations and satanic prayers over me, my family, and my ministry in the name of Jesus.

18. In the name of Jesus, I command that this day be taken back from my enemies' grasp.

19. I command that every battle in the heavens be won in favor of the angels conveying my blessings today.

20. I decree that whatever I bind or loose on earth is already bound or loosed in heaven.

21. I command that revelation, healing, deliverance, salvation, peace, joy, Godly relationships, finances, and Godly resources that may have been blocked by hostile forces be released to me now.

22. I declare that I am abundantly blessed, and my blessing is infectious.

23. I command the sun, moon, and stars to carry all afflictions back to their sender(s) in the name of Jesus.

24. My God, arise and uproot everything that is working against me today.

25. I declare that all harmful aspects be removed from my life immediately.

26. I demand that malice, cruelty, or immorality be eliminated so my loved ones and I can live and prosper in a tranquil and thriving environment.

27. You, sun, as you come forth, I command that you uproot all the wickedness against me, my family, and my ministry.

28. I command the sun, moon, stars, earth, and waters to be programmed with blessing for my life today.

Prayers To Condition My Day

29. I command the sun to cancel every daily evil program drawn against me, my family, and my ministry.

30. I command the sun to torment every enemy of the kingdom of God in my life today.

31. I demand the removal of any negative influence in my life. Let them be banished forever and never cross my path again.

32. You evil one, I decree that you shall not hurt me today.

33. I stand firm in my spiritual authority and declare that my adversaries will not take anything from me, my loved ones, or my ministry today.

34. I establish the power of God over my life in the name of Jesus.

35. I command you, sun, moon, and stars, to fight against the stronghold of witchcraft targeted against me, my family, and my ministry.

36. I command the heavens to torment all my unrepentant enemies to submission today, in the name of Jesus.

37. I release the heavens to kill the stronghold of witchcraft, fighting me, my family, and my ministry.

38. I command that every unholy altar in the heavens be thrown to the ground and shatter into irreparable pieces in the name of Jesus.

39. I command that all negative influence or harm directed toward myself, my loved ones, and my ministry be eradicated.

40. I command every evil pattern in the heavens to be broken.

41. My God, arise and destroy every astral altar affecting me and my loved ones.

42. I command that every satanic connection between the heavens and my birthplace be destroyed in Jesus's name.

43. I command the immediate disgracing of every spiritual wickedness in the heavens that will reinforce against me today.

44. Thus saith the lord, let no principality, power, ruler of darkness, spiritual wickedness trouble me today, for I bear in my body the marks of the Lamb of God.

45. I pull down every dark power hidden in the heavens against me today; not only do I pull you down, but I command you to die by fire or by force in the name of Jesus.

46. I bring down any evil power floating or hanging in the heavens against me; I trample you under my feet.

47. I command the sun, moon, and stars to favor me, my family, and my ministry today.

48. I declare I will find favor with both God and man today.

49. Every evil arrangement prepared by the sorcerers and witches against my life today, I command them to scatter and die in the name of Jesus.

50. Any evil thing that has been or will be programmed into the sun, the moon, and the stars against my life, my family, and my ministry today is dismantled in the name of Jesus.

51. I command every negative thing written in the moon cycle against me, my family, and my ministry today to be blotted out by the power of the blood of Jesus.

52. I command that every season of frustration and failure be shaken off my life, family, and ministry.

53. I command the immediate dismantling of every satanic agenda for my life.

Commanding My Morning

54. I decree that every evil word programmed against my star in the heavens shall not be established in Jesus' name.

55. I terminate every evil agreement between my enemies and the heavens.

56. Every evil handwriting programmed by satanic agents into the heavens against my life, I command them to be wiped out by the blood of Jesus.

57. I retrench and frustrate every satanic priest ministering enchantment into the sun, the moon, and the stars against my life, against my family, and my ministry in Jesus' name.

58. I command there be a complete and total retrieval of any of my properties dedicated to the sun, the moon, the stars, and the elements by the power of darkness.

59. You heavens, I command you to refuse to give a reply to any satanic programming against my life, my family, and my ministry in Jesus' name.

60. I overthrow every evil war fought against me in the heavens.

61. Every power programming evil into my star, I command you to fall and die in Jesus' name.

Prayers To Condition My Day

62. My Lord, cause my whole heart to rest as I trust You completely today.

63. My Lord, let my fellowship with You become greater today.

64. I stand against every satanic operation that would hinder my prayers today.

65. Every wicked spirit planning to rob me of the will of God, I command you to fall and die in the name of Jesus.

66. Today, I tear down the stronghold of satan against my life, family, and ministry.

67. Every diabolical power cursing my destiny into ineffectiveness, I bind you now!

68. I strike down every evil force siphoning my blessing with chaos and confusion in the name of Jesus.

69. I nullify the incantations of evil spiritual consultants in Jesus' name.

70. I turn the wicked devices of witchcraft upside down and command that every unrepentant witch dies by fire. For it is written, suffer a witch not to live.

71. I render every satanic weapon harmless in Jesus' name.

72. Every power cursing my destiny, I command you to be silenced and ineffective.

73. Today, I refuse to be in the right place at the wrong time.

74. I command all of heaven and the elements to facilitate my being at the right place at the right time.

75. I bind every negative energy in the air, water, and ground working against me, my family, and my ministry, in the name of Jesus.

76. Anything from the kingdom of darkness that has made it their business to hinder me, I single you out right now, bind you, cast you out, and cause you to disappear, in the name of Jesus.

77. I command every stubborn spirit fighting God's will for my life, family, and ministry to be bound with chains that cannot be broken.

78. I strip off all my enemy's spiritual armor; I disgrace them; I slay them with the flaming sword of the Lord.

79. I isolate every stubborn spirit; I command that they lose all the support of other evil powers, I weaken them with the ammunitions of the third and first

Prayers To Condition My Day

heavens, and I command them to die by fire; die by fire now!

80. You evil spirit, I bind you and command you not to involve yourself with me again.

81. Let the handwriting of ordinances programmed by satanic agents into the heavens against me be wiped out by the blood of Jesus.

82. I recover all my virtues dedicated to the elements in the name of Jesus.

83. I command the heavens and the elements to turn against every satanic programmer in the name of Jesus.

84. I command the heavens to declare the glory of God over my life in the name of Jesus.

85. Every evil thing programmed into my life in the heavens, I dismantle you, in the name of Jesus.

86. I command the spirits of favor, counsel, might, and power to come upon me now.

87. I declare that I shall excel today, and nothing shall defile me in the name of Jesus.

88. I shall possess the gates of my enemies today in the name of Jesus.

89. I declare that the Lord has anointed me with the oil of gladness above my enemies.

90. I decree that the enemy's fire will not burn me, my family, and my ministry today.

91. I command my ears to hear good news and refuse to listen to the enemy's voice today.

92. I command all the works of the hands of God to ensure that my life and family are secured in Christ Jesus.

93. I command that angels with flaming swords dismantle every satanic checkpoint mounted against me in the heavens.

94. I command every evil altar prepared against my breakthroughs in the heavens to be destroyed by fire.

95. You spiritual wickedness in the heavens militating against my star, I bring the hook of the Lord against you, I frustrate your activities, I strip away all of your powers, I render you ineffective, I command you to die.

96. Today, I cover myself, my family, and my ministry with divine insurance against all forms of accident and tragedy.

Prayers To Condition My Day

97. I send lightning, thunder, and the hook of the Lord against the evil kings and queens in the heavens militating against me, my family, and my ministry.

98. I command a change to every evil spiritual equation programmed against my life, family, and my ministry.

99. I declare that the headquarters of evil programmers be destroyed and their altars demolished in the name of Jesus.

100. I command anything drawing power against me from the heavens to fall and die, in the name of Jesus.

101. Oh Lord, I ask that today, you give me the ability equal to my opportunity.

102. Lord, I ask you to empower me to harvest the fruits of success.

103. Oh God, I ask that you empower me to reach my goal today.

104. Oh Lord, I ask that you guide my words today and let them bear fruits.

105. Oh Lord, Please give me divine alertness to recognize divine opportunities.

106. I declare that I am releasing spermatic words that make contact with the morning's womb, making her pregnant with my commandments.

107. I further declare that my daily testimony will be accurate and speedy deliveries of favor and blessings.

108. I command that at sunrise, the dawn gives birth to the will of God, and light shines on wickedness to shake it from the heavens.

109. I command that my enemies flee at sunrise, and their spoils await me at my destination.

110. I declare that my destiny is inevitable!

111. As I command the morning and capture the day, I decree that time is being redeemed in my favor.

112. I command that the atmosphere of the airways over me, my family, church, community, nation, and the world is producing a new climate. This new climate is constructing Godly Strongholds for my family, church, community, and government.

113. Today, I command that people's thinking will be conducive to the agenda of the Kingdom of Heaven for my life.

Prayers To Condition My Day

114. I command that every demonic agenda or evil thought pattern designed against the plan of God is destroyed at the root of conception, in Jesus' name!

115. I agree with the saints, as we have suffered violence; even now, I decree that we are taking back what rightfully belongs to us by force!

116. In the name of Jesus, I declare that I will no longer accept anything dealt to me by the enemy; but I command that from this day onwards, God's will dictates my days for my life.

117. Today, I command the sun to shine favorably upon me, my family, and my ministry.

118. I decree that God's protection and provision are my portions today because I have no thought for tomorrow.

119. I am now riding on the wings of the morning into my day of victory in the name of Jesus.

120. God, I ask that you separate the night and the day to declare my days, years, and seasons.

121. I decree that I am the light of the earth, and I have been separated from darkness.

Commanding My Morning

122. I decree that the Lord has given me dominion over the elements and all the work of His hands, and God has placed them under my feet.

123. Because I fear the name of the Lord, the Sun of Righteousness arises with my healing in His wings.

124. I will continue to tread down the wicked until they become ashes.

125. I commit to walking in dominion today.

126. I decree and declare a new day, a new season and a fresh anointing has come for me, my family, and my ministry.

127. I command the ordinances of the constellation to manifest what I command.

128. I bind every force attempting to capture my destiny today with the blood of Jesus Christ.

129. I plead the blood of Jesus over every principality, power, ruler of darkness, and spiritual wickedness in high places assigned against my purpose today.

130. I bind every destiny pirate, destiny thief, and destiny devourer in the name of Jesus!

Prayers To Condition My Day

131. I command every evil agent to be dethroned and dismantled and have no influence over my days, in Jesus' name.

132. I command every curse sent against my days to be reversed and boomeranged back to the pits of hell.

133. I command the Luciferian spirit to be displaced in the mighty name of Jesus.

134. I bind every false light bearer and counterfeit son of the morning.

135. I command my prayers to disrupt dark plans and give my enemies a non-prosperous day.

136. I declare that I have victory over my enemies this and every morning.

137. I declare that my days are prosperous because I obey and serve the Lord!

Prayers To Condition My Day

Prayer Points for Praying for Your Child(ren)

1. Father God, I repent of my sins and any iniquities of my past or present that may negatively work against the lives of my child(ren).

2. Lord, I thank you for the salvation, healing, deliverance, and prosperity of (***INSERT NAME OF CHILD or CHILDREN***).

3. I command every secret enemy operating behind the scenes in their lives to be uncovered forever under the spotlight of the Holy Ghost.

4. I command every generational sin in my life and the lives of my ancestors to be disconnected from my child(ren)'s heritage now.

5. I plead the Blood of Jesus over my child(ren)'s navel.

6. I take my authority as their parent/guardian, and I cut off every demonic umbilical cord connected to my child(ren).

7. I command that all evil inheritances that rebelliously flow through my bloodline are cut off from my child(ren) forever.

8. I command the blessings of the Lord to flow to my child(ren).

9. I decree that no curses shall touch my child(ren).

10. I declare that the Destiny Angel of the Lord displaces all destiny-devouring spirits assigned to my child(ten).

11. I decree that I now walk in the authority that Jesus has given me over my child(ren).

12. I break the powers of negative peer pressure and ungodly associations over my child(ren), in the name of Jesus.

13. I prophesy that my child(ren) will be great leaders, not followers.

14. I declare that my child(ren) is/are not bound and influenced by the "spirit of the world."

15. I command every vicious cycle ruling over my child(ren) head through association, incantation, or generational influence, to be destroyed by the whirlwind of the Lord.

16. I command that all self-inflicted curses through negative confessions be broken over my child(ren)'s life/lives.

17. I command all negative words spoken over my child(ren) through ignorance or intention be erased now by the precious blood of Jesus.

18. I command all doors that have illegally or legally made way for any demonic activity to operate in my child(ren)'s lives to be closed forever.

19. Even now, I uproot every seed planted in my child(ren)'s life/lives while they slept.

20. I now plead the Blood of Jesus over my child(ren) as they sleep.

21. I command sweet sleep and divine rest upon them.

22. In the name of Jesus, I command the immediate binding of incubus, succubus, and all other perversions trying to affect my child(ren)'s life.

23. I take authority over the terrors that come by night and declare that as the sun rises, it shines favor upon my child(ren).

24. I come against every evil entry point through a nightmare or dark vision through astral activity; I command that they are closed forever, in the name of Jesus.

25. I decree that the will of God has captured my child(ren)'s days.

26. I prophesy that (**INSERT CHILD NAME**) will fulfill the call of the Lord and be called Blessed.

27. I decree that princes, powers, and spiritual wickedness in high places have no dominion over my child(ren).

28. I decree prosperous spiritual airways over my child(ren) heads, and they will live full and Godly lives.

29. I declare that the statistics of the children of the world will not be the statistics of my child(ren) because they are the child(ren) of the light.

30. I prophesy that the countenances of my child(ren) shine above the countenances of the children of the world.

31. I confess that my child(ren) is/are in the world but not of the world.

32. I command the wealth of the wicked to find its way to my child(ren) now.

33. I declare that my child(ren) possesses the gates of their enemies and displaces them in the name of Jesus.

34. I declare that the god of the cosmos cannot prosper against my child(ren) in the mighty name of Jesus Christ.

35. I prophesy that my children can discern the difference between what is holy and unholy and that they will forever choose what is holy.

36. I command that boarders be enlarged unto my child(ren); and that they will rise and demand room to live, in the name of Jesus!

37. I decree that rebellion, disobedience, and unbelief have no rule over my child(ren).

38. Even now, I circumcise my child(ren) with a sharp knife (the Word of the Lord) and pull them out of the ways of the uncircumcised, in Jesus' name.

39. I decree that my child(ren) is/are wealthy, wise, and in the place to receive from God.

40. I command that the words I speak over them also affect their child(ren).

41. I decree that sickness, disease, accidents, incidents, or the cares of the world shall not prematurely kill my child(ren).

42. I command that my child(ren) live long, prosperous lives and serve God eternally because this is the heritage of my seed for a thousand generations.

43. I command that these words are forever programmed in the heavens; in Jesus' name, Amen!

Prayers To Condition My Day

Welcome to our Family

At Faith & Works Ministries, our mission is to reveal and teach individuals the transformative power of biblical principles that can impact every aspect of their lives. By fostering a deep understanding and personal application of these principles, we can empower individuals to lead more fulfilling and meaningful lives marked by faith, purpose, and service to God and others.

Another aspect of our mission is to empower individuals to combine their faith with works in a way that brings hope and transformation to their communities and the world. Through our various ministry programs and outreach efforts, we strive to create opportunities for people to put their faith into action, serving God and others with compassion and grace.

Faith and works go hand in hand and are essential in becoming what and whom God has intended us to become. We are committed to living out our faith through meaningful actions and services within our church community and the world. We recognize that our faith is not just something we profess with our words but is demonstrated through the love and care we show God and others.

Through engaging worship experiences, relevant teaching, and compassionate care, we seek to create a welcoming and inclusive community where all people can grow in their relationship with God and discover their unique gifts and calling. For more information, visit www.faithandworks.church.

Made in the USA
Columbia, SC
11 July 2023